Ireland

For all the children in the world. May you forever stay curious about the world around you - K.J.

Sloth Dreams Publishing
Published by Sloth Dreams Publishing
Sloth Dreams Children's Books
Pennsylvania, USA

http://www.SlothDreams.com/kids

My Country

by KeriAnne N. Jelinek

Ireland

www.SlothDreams.com

Ireland is on the continent of Europe. Europe is not a country. Europe is a continent.

A continent is a large mass of land that has many different countries within it. Each country is entirely unique and different from any other country. Each and every country has its own foods, language, culture, music and traditions.

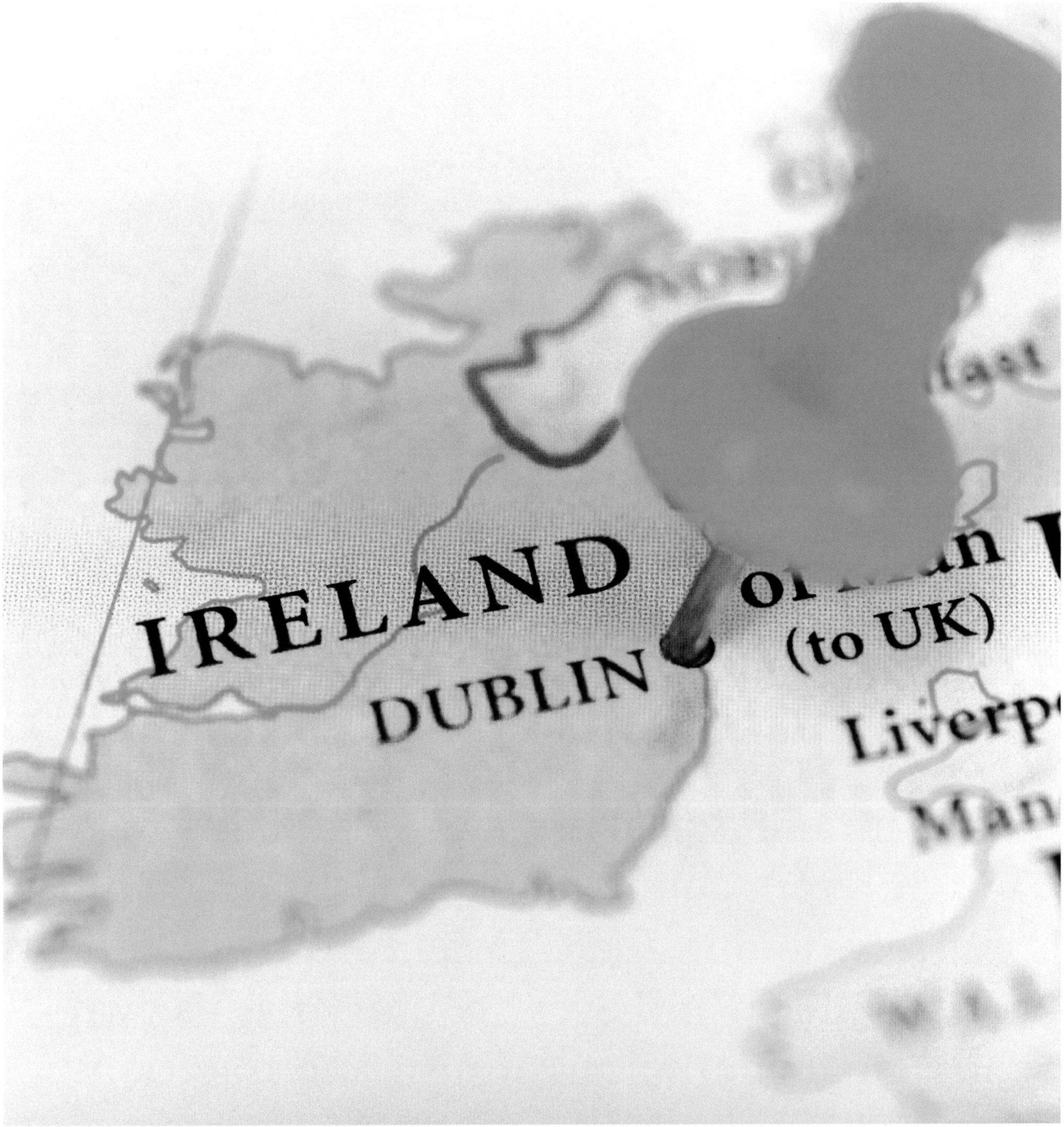
IRELAND
DUBLIN
(to UK)

Ireland is a country that is about the
size of Indiana in the United States.

From north to south is 302 Miles long
and from east to west is 171 miles wide.

Indiana, USA   Ireland, EU

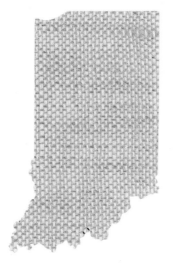   

To the North, South and West of Ireland lies the Atlantic Ocean. To the East lies the beautiful Irish Sea.

Ireland is an island country completely surrounded by water.

The Capital of Ireland is Dublin. It is the largest city in Ireland. Cork, Limerick, Galway and Belfast are all cities in Ireland.

The National Flag is often called the "tricolour" or *Bratach na heireann.* It has vertical stripes of green, orange and white.

Green was intended to stand for the inclusion and peace between the Catholic people and the Protestants, symbolized by the orange color. The white in the middle of the flag signified a lasting peace between the two religious groups.

The two main religions of Ireland are Catholic and Protestant. Saint Patrick is the patron saint who is credited with bringing Christianity to Ireland.

Saint Patrick, the patron saint of Ireland, is one of the most famous people in Irish culture.

There are many legends about Saint Patrick. The most famous story is how he banished all the snakes out of Ireland. Whether it is true, nobody knows.

Saint Patrick used the clover to teach Christianity to the people of Ireland.

St. Patrick's Day, named for the patron Saint Patrick, is the holiday that is celebrated each year on March 17.

St. Patrick's Day is the Irish holiday that commemorates Saint Patrick with religious services and feasts.

The celebration, in the United States, has transformed into a mostly secular holiday. It is celebrated by wearing green, wearing clover, eating corned beef and cabbage. Many cities around the United States have St. Patrick's Day parades. Many cities also dye their river's green in celebration of Irish heritage.

Some of the common foods eaten in Ireland include: potatoes, Irish stew, fish, bacon and cabbage, boxty (potato pancakes), soda bread, corn beef and cabbage and shepherd's pie.

Ireland has many farms. The top farms produce beef, milk and potatoes. Irish crops also include Barley, Oats and Wheat.

Dairy farms and raising sheep for wool is a large part of Irish production today. Ireland produces some of the best cheeses and wool in the world. Irish wool is some of the world's finest.

Weather in Ireland is often damp, cold, cloudy and rainy throughout most of the year. The average temperatures are around 50 - 55 degrees Fahrenheit.

Traditional Irish clothing are made from Irish wool. Men wear kilts. Women wear leine. Kilts and lein's are traditional clothing of the Irish people. Certain colors and patterns mean they belong to a certain Irish heritage called a Clan.

Irish clans are traditional groups based on kinship or family heritage. Clans usually share a common last name or a group of last names. Clans usually mean the groups are somehow related to one another.

The official languages of Ireland are
Gaelic and English.

Ireland's official money is the Euro. The Irish Pound was the money of Ireland until January 1, 1999, when the Euro replaced it.

Euros

Irish Pounds

The people of Ireland typically have fair skin, a variety of hair colors from brown to red, and blue, green, hazel and brown eyes.

The red-haired Irish have different genes called HG1's that are responsible for producing the typical Irish physical traits, such as: freckles, curly hair, red hair and blue eyes. The gene is located on chromosome 7 and it is responsible for creating this overall Irish look. The Irish red-haired "look" is very common in not only Ireland, but in neighboring countries of Scotland and Wales.

Special landmarks are not only tourist attractions, but special monuments to the Irish people's past ancestors and ancestral heritage.

Some of the famous landmarks include: the Blarney Stone and Castle in Cork, Rock of Cashel (Tipperary) also called St. Patrick's Rock, St. Patrick's Cathedral in Dublin, Giant's Causeway (Antrim) a natural stone wonder, and the Cliff's of Moher (Clare) that boast awe inspiring sea cliffs.

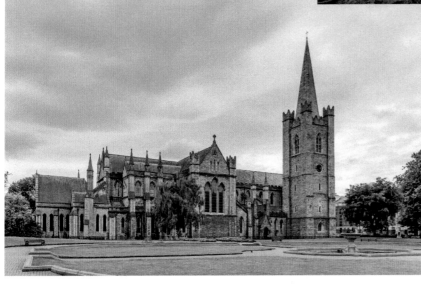

The shamrock is Ireland's national plant. The four-leaf clover in ancient Celtic tradition's was said to bring good luck and prosperity. To this day, four leaf clovers are rare and still are considered to bring good luck to people all around the world.

Ireland's national bird is the Northern Lapwing.

Ireland's national animal is a Red deer.

Ireland's national dog breed is the Irish Wolfhound.

This is an Irish Setter breed of dog that originated in Ireland. It has a beautiful red coat and long sleek hair.

It is a very popular breed worldwide.

Irish Dance, often called Celtic Dance, is a very popular dance for children, teens and adults alike.

Some of the most popular dances are called reels, jigs and slip jigs.

The soft shoe, a ballet-like slipper, is called the Ghillies, and the tap-shoe like dance shoe is called the hard shoe or Heavies.

Irish dancers, often called, Celtic Dancers, wear traditional Irish costumes and curly Irish hair pieces when they dance.

The most common musical instruments of Ireland are the: Violin (fiddle), Irish Harp, Bodhran Drum, Uilleann Pipes (bagpipes), Celtic wood flutes and various tin whistles.

There are some very famous musicians that come from Ireland. *Celtic Woman* is an international group of musicians that tour the world and are very famous. *Riverdance* (Lord of the Dance), *Enya, The Dubliners, U2, The Cranberries, Sinead O'Connor, Bono, The Irish Rovers, Flogging Molly* and many more famous musicians come from Ireland.

From classical and traditional music to New Age and other popular genres of music, Ireland has musicians and music of every style.

Ireland's ancient stone circles are a form of stone art that dates back to 600 BC. Pictured below is *Dromberg Stone Circle*. It is a megalithic site that is the most visited in all of Ireland.

The Celtic Cross is a famous symbol of Ireland. The art dates back to the early Middle Ages. These symbols became very popular in the 12th Century Ireland.

The famous art of Ireland can also be seen in its beautiful jewelry.

Many Irish symbols appear in jewelry, paintings, and in Irish architecture.

Ireland has many castles that date back to the 11th and 12th centuries. There are over 30,000 castles and castle ruins in Ireland alone.

The most well know are Bunratty Castle and Blarney Castle.

Some famous artists who come from Ireland are: Sir John Lavery (Portrait Painter), Jack Butler Yeats (Oil Painter), Anna Doran (Muralist), and Louis le Brocquy (Cubist Painter).

Sir John Lavery

Jack Butler Yeats

Anna Doran

Louis Le Brocquy

Study for Samuel Beckett, 1979 -
Louis le Brocquy

The Fighting Dawn, 1945 - Jack Butler Yeats

The Chess Players, 1929 - Sir John Lavery

Waterford Walls, 2015 - Anna Doran

Ireland has a grand heritage of myths and fairytales. Leprechauns, fairies, Pooka, butterflies, selkies and shape shifters are all a part of a rich culture of storytelling.

Selkies meaning 'Seal Folk' are Celtic and Norse mythological beings capable of changing from seal form into human form by shedding their seal skin. They are often young girls or young boys.

Leprechauns in Irish folklore are small fairy-like supernatural beings. They are usually depicted as little men with beards, wearing a coat and hat, and usually partaking in mischief and tomfoolery.

There are many famous actors and actresses that come from Ireland. Liam Neeson, Colin Farrell, Pierce Brosnan, Aidan Turner, Saoirse Ronan and Evanna Lynch are just a few of the most well know movie stars that come from Ireland.

Liam Neeson

Evanna Lynch

Colin Farrell

Aidan Turner

Saoirse Ronan

Pierce Brosnan

Some of the most famous prolific literary writers came from Ireland. James Joyce and Oscar Wilde are two of the world's greatest writers and most well read authors in the world.

Oscar Wilde

James Joyce

Ireland is a country of great beauty. It is a country of grand traditions and cultural heritage. The people of Ireland are charming, kind, tolerant, warm with a little bit of stubborn thrown in.

Ireland, is often called the "*Emerald Isle*" because of its hillsides of green. Its many natural resources, history and art make it an ideal country to visit.

Perhaps one day you will be so lucky as to experience the beauty, culture, people and everything that Ireland has to offer. Keep on traveling!